ALLIANCE FOR THE ARTS IN RESEARCH UNIVERSITIES

Copyright © 2019 by the Regents of the University of Michigan

Some rights reserved

This work is licensed under the Creative Commons Attribution-ShareAlike 4.0 International Public License.

To view a copy of this license, visit http://creativecommons.org/licenses/by-sa/4.0/ or send a letter to Creative Commons, PO Box 1866, Mountain View, California, 94042, USA.

Published in the United States of America by
Michigan Publishing

DOI: https://doi.org/10.3998/mpub.11660546

ISBN: 978-1-60785-628-3 (paper)
ISBN: 978-1-60785-629-0 (open-access)

A2RU PARTNER UNIVERSITIES

Boston University
Carnegie Mellon University
Dartmouth College
James Madison University
Johns Hopkins University
Kent State University
Louisiana State University
Massachusetts Institute of Technology
Michigan State University
Northeastern University
Oregon State University
Penn State
Pontificia Universidad Católica de Chile
Princeton University
Rochester Institute of Technology
Texas Tech University
Tufts University
The University of Alabama
The University of Alabama at Birmingham
University of Arizona
University of Arkansas

University of California, Berkeley
University of Cincinnati
University of Colorado Boulder
University of Colorado Denver
University of Florida
University of Georgia
University of Houston
University of Illinois at Urbana-Champaign
University of Iowa
University of Kansas
University of Maryland
University of Michigan
University of Nebraska-Lincoln
University of Nevada, Las Vegas
University of North Texas
University of Texas at Dallas
University of Utah
University of Virginia
University of Wisconsin-Madison
Virginia Commonwealth University
Virginia Tech

The Alliance for the Arts in Research Universities (a2ru) is a partnership of over 40 institutions committed to ensuring the greatest possible institutional support for the full spectrum of arts and arts-integrative research, curricula, programs, and creative practice for the benefit of all students and faculty at research universities and the communities they serve.

IMPACTS OF ARTS INTEGRATION & INTERDISCIPLINARY PRACTICE

A2RU Research to Practice

Where the arts have a lively presence on campus, and interact with other disciplines as well as across the boundaries of the university, we find a range of impacts. Some of them are high-level—recurring and broadly applicable—while others are specific to a particular group or field. This report presents a synthesis of our research findings on the ways that arts and interdisciplinary practice in the university lead to new perspective, new awareness, and new understanding. Companion reports recount the impacts we found in other areas and for other populations.

Our taxonomy of impacts is built on examples that surfaced from interview and survey data, and on a review of the literature. Some impacts are verified with experimental studies and some are anecdotal or aspirational; thus, we consider this a taxonomy of the potential impacts of arts integration in the university. Two extensive studies form the basis of our research: in a series of interviews with academic leadership, faculty, and students at 38 universities, we asked about the impact of their arts-integration initiatives, including teaching, research, and community projects. In addition, a four-year survey-based longitudinal study explored ~4000 undergraduates' arts engagement at the University of Michigan. For more information about how results from these two studies are integrated with relevant literature, see Methodology, pages 32-35; you can find notes on how the different sources are cited on pages 30-31.

In addition to reports like this one, our insights into the impacts data are available as a graphic map (the images on the cover and on page 5 are excerpted from it). Each type of resource has a distinctive function. Readers can use the map for a broad overview of the impacts taxonomy, browsing for categories of impact that interest them; alternatively, the reports go deeper into the research, discussing some impacts in detail and providing specific examples of many types of impact. The map and reports are meant to ignite discussion, fuel research, and support clear communication. We encourage users to appropriate the taxonomy for advocacy and case-making, as a locator guide to identify where impacts can occur, and as a shared reference point and vocabulary for pursuing arts-integrative initiatives in the university. However, it is most exciting as a jumping-off point to further exploration.

https://www.a2ru.org/projects/impacts/

New Perspective, Awareness, and Understanding

Arts-integrated teaching, research, and community-engaged activities find people with expertise in the arts working together with those whose expertise is in other fields. As a result, everyone involved experiences the shared work from a new perspective. Those new perspectives, practically by definition, constitute fertile ground for learning; we re-examine what we thought we knew in light of the new, with the possibility that our understanding will need to be taken apart and rebuilt. The twenty sub-categories of *New Perspective, Awareness, and Understanding* explore related but distinct aspects of such encounters. They recur across the impacts landscape, affecting a wide range of people and practices, and amplifying learning and conceptual change writ large.

A Jumping-off Point for Exploration

In our analysis of arts integration in the university, we organized categories of impact into a structure wherein the categories have relationships to each other. While that structure is more cyclical than linear, in narrating it here, we need an entry point—a beginning for the story. Our account of the impacts begins then with the convergence of two forces, or concepts: the arts and interdisciplinarity. These are the component parts of arts integration. The immediate result, felt by those participating in arts-integrative teaching, research, or community engagement is correspondingly twofold:

Exposure to the Arts. We intend this somewhat reductive shorthand to account for the way experience changes when the arts are present, especially for those who don't usually encounter the arts.

Diverse Thinkers Come Together. This foundational aspect of interdisciplinarity is the other key piece of arts integration; there is broad functional and conceptual diversity.

Two broad categories of impact, *New Perspective, Awareness, and Understanding* and *Working Together*, emerge directly out of this arts-integrative situation. These impacts are pervasive and recurring. They are active wherever arts integration impacts are felt—on a specific discipline, in the classroom, or outside the university entirely—and they take on differing characteristics in each situation. For many, these impacts—including thinking beyond disciplinary boundaries, new understanding, and bringing together diverse thinkers—are at the heart of arts integration.

Other broad impacts include the emergence of a *Unique Way of Knowing, Involvement and Enthusiasm, High-Quality and Innovative Work,* and *Prestige and Recognition.*

We also identified impacts on specific areas. Impacts on academia affect *Teaching, Research, The University* itself, and individual *Disciplines*. These impacts flow to *Students*. The students become agents of impact outside the university, but there are also other direct impacts on the *World Outside the University,* often because of publicly engaged scholarship.

This report addresses only the *New Perspective, Awareness, and Understanding* category, unpacking it and defining its many sub-categories. Other reports explore the other impacts, both broad and specific.

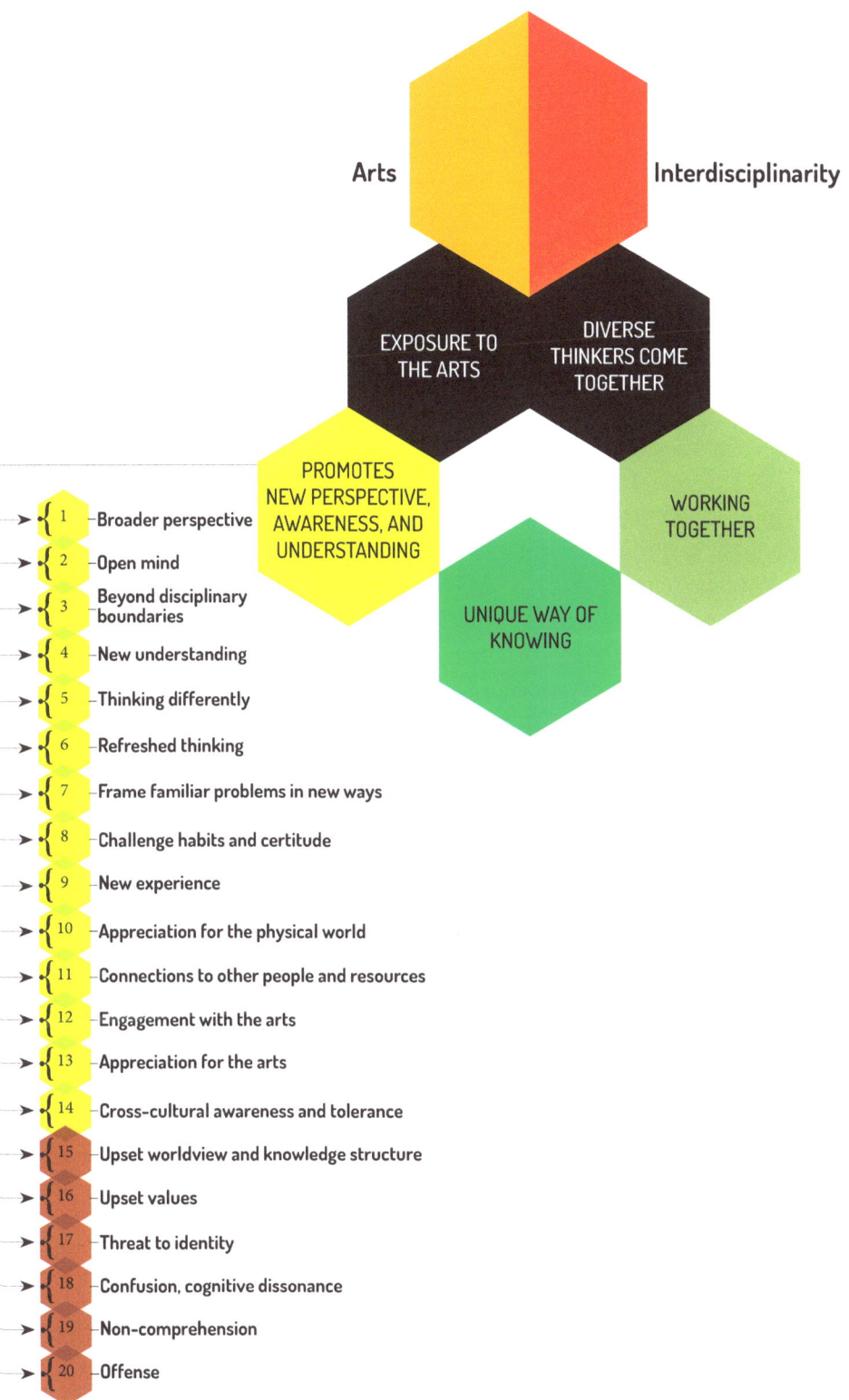

Exploring New Perspectives

New Perspective, Awareness, and Understanding has multiple sub-categories, many ways in which the main idea is refracted or manifests in slightly different ways. What these many manifestations have in common is the idea of encounter with something unfamiliar—not just unfamiliar concepts, but unfamiliar ways of thinking about concepts.

Such an encounter with new perspectives, practically by definition, constitutes fertile ground for learning. One broadly accepted theory of learning stipulates that, cognitively, we structure knowledge into schemata or frameworks of understanding. When presented with new information, we either assimilate it into these schemata, or we modify the schemata to accommodate the new information. (Piaget, Piery, and Berlyne 1950; Sternberg 2002). The notion of accommodation implies that, contrary to an additive view of learning wherein we have a bank of knowledge to which we add new deposits, acquiring new knowledge changes the knowledge that was already there. We must re-examine what we thought we knew in light of the new, with the possibility that it will need to be taken apart and rebuilt. Where, for example, science and the arts are integrated, we find this sort of conceptual de- and reconstruction. In many sample cases, scientists and artists not only learn about each other's fields, they reconfigure what they know about their own fields, based on the other's perspective of it (Gurnon, Voss-Andreae, and Stanley 2013; Jeffries 2011; Stevens and O'Connor 2017; Tambiah and Lamberts 2011).

The category *New Perspective, Awareness, and Understanding* is notable then for several reasons. It refracts into many related but distinct experiences; it recurs across the impacts landscape, affecting a wide range of people and practices; and it coincides substantially with learning in general.

Sarah Sze's "Timekeeper" at the Rose Art Museum at Brandeis University (2016).
SARAH SZE AND TANYA BONAKDAR GALLERY

BIG-PICTURE PERSPECTIVE

Through the encounter with difference inherent in arts integration and interdisciplinarity—working with people from disparate disciplines, in perhaps unfamiliar modes—people gain a newfound understanding of the "big picture." They acquire a more expansive sense of the world or of themselves, which some see as an integral part of a university education. This broader perspective can be undefined, or can specifically entail thinking beyond the limits of one's own discipline. All of these experiences have as their prerequisite a willingness, an availability, an open mind.

BROADER PERSPECTIVE

"With my outreach project, for example, it started out as attempting to give my students something that gave them some perspective." (Q25-2113-528)

"The impact that I was hoping to see was that students have a very broad understanding of what it means to be an educated, good human person." (Q25-1401-4413)

"If we're not titillated by certain types of textures and things, if we don't understand those things, we don't have a real understanding of the world. If arts aren't integrated into education, how are people going to have a broad sense and true understanding of the world?" (Q25-1401-4416)

"Arts have always been a part of the general education requirement, so the university sees that appreciation of getting a broader-based view of the world." (Q25-4002-6530)

"The arts can expand your thinking by increasing range of knowledge and allowing one to evaluate more opinions." (UM-AE: In what ways do you think you can grow through the arts?)

OPEN MIND

"I think the arts will help me to stay open to new ways of thinking and new experiences. To me, the arts are a reminder that life does not have to be mundane or routine but can be sublime and wonderful as well." (UM AE: In what ways do you think you can grow through the arts?)

"I'm a civil engineer and often spend the majority of my time thinking analytically and technically. My exposure to the arts has been a nice contrast, opening up my mind to a whole new way of thinking/ expression." (UM-AE: How did your involvement in the arts during college make you feel?)

BIG-PICTURE PERSPECTIVE

BEYOND DISCIPLINARY BOUNDARIES

"It's more of a long-term thing, in terms of getting people to think outside of their narrow discipline and getting them to think a bit more broadly." (Q25-4019-6875)

"We have to constantly challenge what our built and visual environment means to the health of a society, to the advancement of a society and culture." (Q25-3804-1072)

"You know artists who don't know about literature or haven't read novels or haven't read poetry, who haven't travelled to foreign countries. And lots of those kinds of things students are introduced to at the university. Then they come to realize that thinking about a structure of a novel could be like thinking about the narrative development in a piece of sculpture." (Q25-3605-8049)

"It definitely has helped me to see the decision makings for teaching, or to make choices in a more holistic way, or to see that from a different perspective than only from a certain discipline perspective" (Q26-2617-3860)

"I expected more people to understand that arts and science are connected…If we transform this building, it would be great that other people just by walking through, without teaching, gain the awareness of art and science." (Q25-2515-5205)

NEW UNDERSTANDING AND NEW THINKING

The arts-integrative or interdisciplinary encounter with difference also imparts new knowledge, which in turn can change ways of thinking.

NEW UNDERSTANDING

"I'm also interested in new lucrative ideas and knowledge. I'm a voracious learner and...I feel like it's [collaboration] an expansive way to learn about the world." (Q25-3002-4554)

"One goal of [this interdisciplinary] course is to have students understand frequency content of sound, and extend this understanding to other areas, including electronics and radar." (Q25-3406-769)

THINKING DIFFERENTLY

"The lab feeds my interest. I learn more things, I try new things; I make things differently because of it. I see the world differently." (Q26-3002-4560)

"I like to take content that I don't know very much about, that I can really study in a variety of different ways, and see what happens to my creative process when I bring that into it and try to make something with it." (Q26-3705-8321)

"It just gives you a broader mindset and makes you think about things in many different ways." (UM-AE: In what ways do you think you can grow through the arts?)

NEW UNDERSTANDING AND NEW THINKING

REFRESHED THINKING

"It mostly affects my research by allowing me, in my very quiet moments during the semester, to question and alter the way that I think." (Q26-4025-7039)

"The arts provided a space for sanity and creative problem-solving. A nice escape from academic and business-related works, while still building professional, positive, and useful life skills." (UM-AE: What role did the arts play in your college experiences, both positive and negative?)

FRAME FAMILIAR PROBLEMS IN NEW WAYS, CHALLENGE HABITS AND CERTITUDE

These categories are identified in the report *Art as a Way of Knowing* (McDougall, Bevan, and Semper 2011), and many of the SPARC examples fit well with them.

"I started reading a lot of books that are outside of my realm, and then what they say about creativity, I put together things that you wouldn't think that they go together. I guess in that sense, I have become a bit more of a risk taker [in my research]." (Q26-2501-4984)

NEW EXPERIENCES

Perspective and understanding are changed not only through thinking; they are also deeply affected by doing. The embodied experience of arts integration contributes significantly to its impact, most noticeably when participants develop an explicit appreciation for that physical experience. Alternatively, these experiences can lead to new acquaintances; people get connected to more and different kinds of other people, which in turn leads to more new experiences.

NEW EXPERIENCE

"[My course gives students] an appreciation for the challenges of physically making things, especially in the digital world…For example, a couple of years ago, I was teaching Vector Calculus—a whole class of engineers, and I said lightheartedly, 'We're going to have cake because it's relevant for integrations about slicing.' You get a round cake and a rectangular cake, and of course you slice a rectangular cake into rectangles and the round cake in wedges, and then you make a point that if you're integrating over a sphere you want wedges. Anyway, so I just said, 'We'll have cake,' and they said, 'Cake? Why?' So I said off the cuff to one of the students, 'You can make the cake,' and this is a 20-year-old engineer, and he said, 'I can't make cake.' I said, 'First of all, you can buy the box, and second of all, the joy of cooking exists for people like you.' I thought that was very odd: well, here's an engineer, he's going to be building bridges. Can't bake a cake." (Q25-2909-1499)

"We can teach tons of people how to use a 3-D printer. A very small percentage will successfully pursue that and do interesting things, do things beyond downloading files and printing someone else's stuff…. if you leave it to a couple of newspaper articles to sum up what 3-D printing is, it's transformed in some way that's not experiential. When you perceive it, if you don't have a first-hand experience with it, you can't engage that conversation intelligently, other than what someone has told you to say about it, based on the group that you're already supposed to be in." (Q25-2411-4113)

NEW EXPERIENCES

APPRECIATION FOR THE PHYSICAL WORLD

"I have asked them, 'Why does art history matter' and their answers are fantastic because they talk about how the art object offers a materiality to the exploration of historical events." (Q25-3604-8027)

"That sort of iterative interplay, and the idea that concept and materiality—or methods of making—are in concert with one another and are being thoughtfully employed as tools is a really important part of our school." (Q25-4111-2921)

CONNECTIONS TO OTHER PEOPLE

"There are just so many people out there. [My collaborator] knows people at Smithsonian that have these huge archives of all the stuff. So he has grants we're hoping to work with my computer science colleagues on… and get this information out to a public with maybe an exhibition at a science museum." (Q26-3704-8293)

"I will also be able to meet new people that are different from the traditional business people I always hang out with and they can give me a different perspective on things." (UM-AE: In what ways do you think you can grow through the arts?)

ENGAGEMENT WITH THE ARTS

Because of arts-integrative and interdisciplinary initiatives, the arts spread out to the world in unconventional forms and unusual places, and as a result, a greater number of people come into contact with the arts. The line between the "exposure" to the arts invoked at the beginning of our story and the "engagement" we see here is a blurry one, but we believe that they are separate valid impacts. We also use the old-fashioned "arts appreciation" here, as a way to infuse the contemporary idea of "arts literacy" with a sense of respect and love.

ENGAGEMENT WITH THE ARTS

"The number of people outside the School of Music who are participating also increases. The re-invitation rate is super high; it's somewhere between 95 and 98 per cent. The number of kids that we reach each year rises." (Q25-4206-908)

"I would hope to see more of that happen, and more people get a chance to enter into the process of becoming more musical, wherever they are in their lives." (Q25-2914-1579)

"In the five years that I've run the film festival...we've almost tripled our attendance during that time. I just think it has been great partnerships within the community so that you broaden your audience base." (Q25-1306-7145)

APPRECIATION FOR THE ARTS

"There's also a selfish motivation in the desire to broaden audiences for our art form. I always feel that any opportunity you can simultaneously reach somebody with this idea and also introduce them to the beauty of chamber music, I'm all over it." (Q25-2307-5914)

"The more one is exposed to the arts and culture, it is a currency. It is a currency that will show up for the rest of your life. No matter what classes you take, no matter where you travel, arts will always come into conversation." (Q25-2404-3988)

PROMOTE CROSS-CULTURAL UNDERSTANDING

The encounter with difference that is inherent in arts integration not only raises awareness of other cultures; it also becomes a means through which other cultures can be understood.

CROSS-CULTURAL UNDERSTANDING

"I've travelled in the country music world and heard this song sung at bluegrass festivals by all-White bands, and heard them talking before and after. And that's my proof that, actually, it got people talking about this thing [lynching], it got people acknowledging this part of the history." (Q25-5201-7803)

One study incorporating arts-based pedagogies into a graduate program in TESOL (Teaching English to Speakers of Other Languages) demonstrates a heightened potential for students' "double vision," creating vibrant Eastern-Western exchanges of intellectual thought and intercultural understanding (Cahnmann-Taylor et al. 2015).

"The arts offer a new lens with which to view different people's experiences and perspectives, and getting a glimpse through that lens can only offer more knowledge about the world and all the people in it." (UM-AE: In what ways do you think you can grow through the arts?)

"You can broaden your horizons and come to appreciate people with different talents and interests, as well as the lives people live in other cultures (even within the same country)." (UM-AE: In what ways do you think you can grow through the arts?)

NEGATIVE IMPACTS

Interviewees refer to new perspective as an entirely positive phenomena. This focus on the positive is probably a function of the sample demographics so, in an effort to provide a more complete representation, we deliberately sought negative impacts of new perspectives. Through a review of literature, we surfaced several potential negative impacts.

These negative impacts are real potential consequences of gaining new perspective or awareness. They can be considered "pain points" in arts integrative practice, and can shut down the process entirely. However, an awareness of these negative impacts affords potentially richer experiences for those involved.

UPSET WORLDVIEW, KNOWLEDGE STRUCTURE, AND VALUES

The literature on education and psychology indicates that the conceptual change required to take on a new perspective or embrace a new understanding does not come easily; there is associated dissonance, discomfort, and loss.

Part of the discomfort is rooted in demands on cognitive economy. Conceptual change is "expensive"; it's difficult to restructure thoughts, and especially so when new concepts are contrary to intuition and habitual ways of thinking. Maintaining the status quo is preferable (Campanario 2002, 1097), whether the new concept is a scientific one or an artistic one; the new perspective that arts integration promises doesn't necessarily come easily or naturally.

New ideas are also risky because they represent disturbances to familiar routines, network relationships, power balances, and even job security (Albrecht and Hall 1991, 274). In fact, we are likely to prefer information that confirms the concepts we are already invested in; taking on new ideas can imply threat to our self-esteem, feelings of being overstrained by high decisional complexity, and associated negative moods (Fischer 2011, 752). Fully adopting a new perspective requires us to rigorously reexamine deeply held values, beliefs, and assumptions (Powell and Kusuma-Powell 2015). This process may be too demanding, leading some to experience the encounter with difference as unpleasant.

Cognitive reframing and upset worldview can be steps along the way to new perspective and understanding, but the dissonance and discomfort associated with them can also stop the process of conceptual change. Then these negative impacts become the end result.

NEGATIVE IMPACTS

THREAT TO IDENTITY

The ideas we embrace are part of our identities. Privately, we are emotionally attached to our ideas, so to abandon them can be painful. Especially in university settings where faculty identify strongly with a single department or field, the ideas they espouse also constitute an important part of their public face. That face might be threatened by a new perspective (Albrecht and Hall 1991, 274). Indeed, new ideas that contradict the ones we hold dear threaten identity on both the private and public planes; if I take on a new perspective, I am not the person I was before. Therefore, it makes sense to reject "knowledge that threatens the self with disintegration" (Carson and Johnston 2000, 80) because even though such knowledge has the potential to be exciting and positive, it also creates dissonance and discomfort around our identities.

CONFUSION, COGNITIVE DISSONANCE, AND NON-COMPREHENSION

Whether the new perspective is that of art or of an unfamiliar discipline, there is always the chance that we simply won't understand. Non-comprehension can drive us to investigate further, seeking answers, but it can also lead to confusion, frustration, and alienation, as we have seen with some students' initial encounters with experimental art. Then, disdain for and rejection of the new perspective are possible outcomes.

OFFENSE

The affront that new perspective presents to our established worldviews can be so severe as to offend us, to make us feel that the ideas we hold dear are disrespected. For example, Andres Serrano's photograph *Piss Christ* offends those with certain views on Catholicism (Fishbein 2012). The perceived insult in offensive ideas not only turns us against those ideas, it also makes us feel attacked, resentful, and angry—a combination of effects that is unlikely to lead to further engagement.

UNDERSTANDING & PRACTICE

FOLLOW-UP: QUESTIONS FOR BUILDING UNDERSTANDING

Identify from your institution three examples of the types of impact in this report.

Identify three examples of these types of impact from somewhere else.

What experiences, methods, and/or practices help impacts related to "new perspectives" emerge?

How do impacts manifest in different ways for different people?

What teaching and learning activities would be relevant for deepening particular impacts in this report?

What kinds of institutional barriers might get in the way of these impacts?

What kinds of incentives or programs could broaden the impacts of arts-integrative teaching, engagement, and/or research?

What counts as evidence for the impacts in this report? What challenges might those who do arts-integrative work face when seeking evidence or justification for these impacts?

UNDERSTANDING & PRACTICE

FUTURE QUESTIONS AND DIRECTIONS FOR RESEARCH

How can we mobilize existing knowledge to broaden our understanding of the impacts of arts integration? What other research overlaps this investigation, allowing the appropriation of relevant findings? What useful perspectives can sociology, psychology, game theory, business, history, and countless other domains lend to this research?

How can we delve deeper into the impacts in this report? How could we establish a causal relationship (not just a correlative one) between arts-integration and a single impact such as "thinking differently"? Could a small-scale longitudinal study go even further, providing not only evidence of causality but even an explanation of how that impact is effected? What other means exist for learning more about the impacts we have discovered?

How can we develop an effective measurement of impact? What tools, methodology, and evidence are appropriate for demonstrating impact? How might new information about the scope or type of impact, obtained through measurement, feed back into the work we do?

How is the picture presented in this report incomplete? What impacts are missing, and where are the gaps? What impacts of arts integration and interdisciplinarity need to be surfaced and addressed?

How else might the impacts data be structured? We have assigned roles and relationships to individual pieces of data and built an organizational structure around them. What are alternative ways to tell the story of the data?

REFERENCES

Albrecht, T.L., and B.J. Hall. 1991. "Facilitating Talk about New Ideas: The Role of Personal Relationships in Organizational Innovation." *Communication Monographs* 58 (3): 273-288.

Cahnmann-Taylor, Melisa, Kuo Zhang, Susan Jean Bleyle, and Yohan Hwang. 2015. "'Searching for an Entrance' and Finding a Two-Way Door: Using Poetry to Create East-West Contact Zones in TESOL Teacher Education." *International Journal of Education & the Arts* 16 (21). https://eric.ed.gov/?id=EJ1084309.

Campanario, Juan Miguel. 2002. "The Parallelism between Scientists' and Students' Resistance to New Scientific Ideas." *International Journal of Science Education* 24 (10): 1095–1110. https://doi.org/10.1080/09500690210126702.

Carson, Terry, and Ingrid Johnston. 2000. "The Difficulty With Difference in Teacher Education: Toward a Pedagogy of Compassion." *Alberta Journal of Educational Research* 46 (1): 75-83. https://journalhosting.ucalgary.ca/index.php/ajer/article/view/54794.

Fishbein, Rebecca. 2012. "'Piss Christ' Photograph Coming To New York, Angering Pols." *Gothamist*. September 22, 2012. https://gothamist.com/2012/09/22/piss_christ_photograph_coming_to_ne.php.

Fischer, Peter. 2011. "Selective Exposure, Decision Uncertainty, and Cognitive Economy: A New Theoretical Perspective on Confirmatory Information Search." *Social and Personality Psychology Compass* 5 (10): 751–62. https://doi.org/10.1111/j.1751-9004.2011.00386.x.

Gurnon, Daniel, Julian Voss-Andreae, and Jacob Stanley. 2013. "Integrating Art and Science in Undergraduate Education." *PLOS Biology* 11 (2): e1001491. https://doi.org/10.1371/journal.pbio.1001491.

Jeffries, Stuart. 2011. "When Two Tribes Meet: Collaborations between Artists and Scientists." *The Guardian,* August 21, 2011, sec. Art and design. http://www.theguardian.com/artanddesign/2011/aug/21/collaborations-between-artists-and-scientists.

McDougall, Marina, Bronwyn Bevan, and Robert Semper. 2011. *Art as a Way of Knowing.* San Francisco, CA: Exploratorium.

Piaget, Jean, Malcolm Piercy, and D. E Berlyne, 1950. *The Psychology of Intelligence.* London: Routledge & Paul.

REFERENCES

Powell, William, and Ochan Kusuma-Powell. 2015. "Overcoming Resistance to New Ideas." *Phi Delta Kappan* 96 (8): 66–69. https://doi.org/10.1177/0031721715583967.

Sternberg, Robert J. 2002. "The Psychology of Intelligence: Jean Piaget." *Intelligence* 30: 482–483. https://doi.org/10.1016/S0160-2896(02)00088-0.

Stevens, Craig, and Gabby O'Connor. 2017. "When Artists Get Involved in Research, Science Benefits." *The Conversation*. August 16, 2017. http://theconversation.com/when-artists-get-involved-in-research-science-benefits-82147.

Tambiah, Charles, and Rod Lamberts. 2011. "Art and Science: Make Love, Not War." *The Conversation*. http://theconversation.com/art-and-science-make-love-not-war-1003.

SOURCE CITATIONS

In-text citations refer readers to the reference list above.

Examples from the SPARC interview data have an in-text citation indicating the unique identifier number of the quotation, but do not appear in the reference list. Each identifier has a prefix that begins with the letter "Q" and a number, indicating the question to which the speaker was responding.

Readers interested in the context for these examples can visit *Supporting practice in the arts, research, and curricula* (SPARC), 2012-2015, in the National Archive of Data on Arts & Culture. https://doi.org/10.3886/ICPSR36823.v1

Examples from the U-M Arts Engagement study also have an in-text citation but do not appear in the reference list. These examples are identified only by the question to which the speaker was responding. As of summer, 2019, the results of the UM Arts Engagement study are under review for publication. Study authors are Gabriel Harp, Debra Mexicotte, Jack Bowman, and Mengden Yuan.

METHODS

IMPACTS RESEARCH: STAGE 1

The insights in this report are based on responses to the following questions in a2ru's SPARC (Supporting Practice in the Arts, Research and Curricula, funded by the Andrew W. Mellon Foundation) interview cycle, which took place 2012-2015.

What impact did you hope to see? What impact did you actually see and how did you measure it? (Question 25)

How have these programs affected your teaching and research? What about your colleagues' teaching and research? [and variations of this wording] (Question 26)

SPARC DATA SAMPLE INFORMATION

The 155 respondents to these two questions were primarily faculty (79%), but also included those in leadership roles at the Director, Dean, and Provost levels (17%), as well as other staff such as curators and librarians. Notably, half of those who identify as Professor also serve in leadership roles. Eighty-eight per cent of those interviewed worked at Research 1 or Research 2 universities, with the remainder at colleges and universities with larger Master's programs, arts-focused four-year schools, and universities with very high research activity.

SPARC interviewees represented disciplinary clusters as follows:

Music, Theatre, and Dance	27%
Fine, Contemporary, and Media Arts	21%
Engineering, Design, Information, and Architecture	18%
Humanities	15%
Natural Sciences and Medicine	10%
Social Sciences, Education, Business, and Law	8%

METHODS

The interviews were recorded and transcribed, and a2ru staff parsed and cleaned the transcripts. There were 212 individual responses in which people talked about a range of experiences—from awards and recognition for innovative research, to strengthened student communities, to sensory gardens for the blind.

From these responses, we tagged every instance in which an interviewee identified an impact of their arts-integrative work and, in the service of distilling this large data set (273 examples), applied a bottom-up coding process. We grouped similar types of impact together, eventually developing a taxonomy of major categories of impact. Since most interviewees did not distinguish between intended and actual impacts, this data set becomes a catalogue of "possible impacts."

We found that the major categories we had identified differ in type. Some center on the object of impact, such as "impact on the community" or "impact on research," and some seem more action-centered, such as "generates involvement and enthusiasm" or "promotes community and collaboration." To make sense of the data, we constructed roles for and relationships among the categories, generating an organizational structure that is fully represented in the comprehensive report on impacts and in the graphic map of impacts, and partially represented in shorter, targeted reports such as this one. Our sense-making, as articulated in this structure, is, of course, inductive and subjective; there are alternative ways of telling the story of this data.

METHODS

IMPACTS RESEARCH: STAGE 2

In 2018, we suplemented and expanded our impacts taxonomy with a literature review and an additional data set — the four-year longitudinal Arts Engagement study of ~4000 undergraduates at the University of Michigan.

In this second phase of our research, we sought broadly to substantiate and expand on what we had found in the SPARC interview data, expecting to add new types of impact to our taxonomy and possibly revise the relationships that we had sketched among impacts. We also specifically looked for negative impacts of arts integration because we suspected that the study sample had led to an over-representation of positive impacts. People participated in the interviews because they were involved in arts integration at their universities. As such, they were likely motivated by a deep commitment to arts integration; quite possibly, they occupied a somewhat counter-cultural space in their department or institution because of the current vanguard status of arts integration in the university. Their inherent commitment, coupled with the possibility that they might often find themselves advocating for or defending arts integration, suggest that when talking to an outside interviewer they would be inclined to emphasize its positive impacts. Indeed, only two of the 273 examples of impact in our initial taxonomy were negative. Recognizing that this is an unrealistic representation, we intentionally looked for negative impacts as part of our literature review.

METHODS

As a result of this supplementary research, we revised some aspects of our structure, including the identity of high-level categories and the relationships among those categories. In addition, we added new sub-categories and examples of impact to our taxonomy. However, readers should note the difference in process between the SPARC research and this supplemental research, and how it manifests in these reports. The original, interview-based research followed a bottom-up process, in which examples—quotations drawn from interviews—formed the foundation. We gathered together examples that were similar in type, and these eventually formed sub-categories, which coalesced into categories. By contrast, with the literature review, we sometimes found categories of impact suggested by research that didn't have accompanying examples (a more top-down approach). Because of this, the reader will notice that some categories of impact are rich with real-life examples while others have theorizing but no examples. Both types serve the goal of the taxonomy—to describe the rich landscape of impacts—even though the narrative representation varies.

ARTS ENGAGEMENT DATA SAMPLE INFORMATION

Interviewees were University of Michigan undergraduate students who responded to questions about the arts in their college experience. This report draws on the following questions from that survey:

In what ways do you think you can grow through the arts?   n=971

How did your involvement in the arts during college make you feel?   n=1207

What role did the arts play in your development as a person, friend, colleague, and student during college?   n=840

PEOPLE

IMPACTS RESEARCH

Research Associate, Contributing Author:
Veronica Dittman Stanich

Research Director, Contributing Author:
Gabriel Harp

A2RU-Mellon SPARC Interviews:
Bruce Mackh and Anthony Kolenic

Arts Engagement Survey:
Deb Mexicotte, PI: the Arts Engagement Project, ArtsEngine

Image Credits: Unless otherwise specified, all image detail is from: Z VIII, 1924 by László Moholy-Nagy, http://www.moholy-nagy.org

www.ingramcontent.com/pod-product-compliance
Lightning Source LLC
LaVergne TN
LVHW010035070426
835507LV00006B/146